Stories of Life

Stories of Life
Written by Dr. Lucius F. Wright

All rights reserved.

Printed and bound in the United States of America. Except as permitted under the U.S. Copyright Act of 1976: Without limiting the rights under copyright reserved above, no part of this publication may be reproduced, stored in or introduced into a retrieval system, or transmitted, in any form, or by any means (electronic, mechanical. photocopying, recording. or otherwise), without the prior written permission of both the copyright owner and the below publisher of this book.

The publisher does not have any control over and does not assume any responsibility for author or third-party Web sites or their content.

The scanning, uploading, and distribution of this book via the Internet or via any other means without the permission of the author or publisher is illegal and punishable by law. Please purchase only authorized electronic editions, and do not participate in or encourage electronic piracy of copyrighted materials. Your support of the author's rights is appreciated.

Copyright © 2014
First Edition – First Printing January 2014
Library of Congress Number pending
ISBN # 978-1-939999-06-1

Published by Main Street Publishing, Inc., Jackson, TN.
Copy Editing by Shari B Hill Yetto
Cover Design by Shari B Hill Yetto
Edited by Dr. Lucius F. Wright - Author
Printed and bound by NetPub, Poughkeepsie, NY.

For more information write Main Street Publishing, Inc.,
206 East Main St., Suite 207, P.O. Box 696, Jackson, TN 38302
Phone 1-731-427-7379 or toll free 1-866-457-7379.
E-mail: editor@mainstreetpublishing.com for managing editor and
lanewble@mainstreetpublishing.com for customer service.
Visit us at www.mainstreetpublishing.com and www.mspbooks.com.

Stories of Life

Lucius F. Wright, M. D.
1721 N. Highland Avenue
Jackson, TN, 38301

Stories of Life

Preface

I have always been interested in stories. Perhaps it began as a child when Dad would take 30 days of leave and we would pack up the car and drive across the country to visit family. The family would sit around and tell stories about other family members for hours. As a child, this often seemed boring, but as an adult I have appreciated how many of those stories stuck in my memory. So it was only natural that I would accumulate stories from the patients I have encountered in my years practicing medicine. I appreciate the privilege of participating in their stories with them as the doctor.

The rise of the computerized medical record has devalued the narrative—now the emphasis is on getting the "bullet points" recorded to support the bill being sent to the insurance company or to Medicare. I fear this emphasis on bullet points will cause us to lose sight of the meaning of what we do, which is usually contained in the narrative.

Since I cannot ask most of these patients for permission to tell their stories, I am using anonymous pronouns. Where that makes telling the tale awkward, I have created aliases. Each story is personal, but the themes are universal. In sharing these stories, I hope you will find them enlightening and even entertaining.

Stories of Life

Chapter 1

Life Stories

Brother Josef was a lay monk at the monastery in Cullman, Alabama, who had been admitted for possible surgery. I was sent to "do a history and physical." Since I was a rookie, he soon took control of the interview by telling me "I almost became a doctor, too." Even as a junior medical student, I had heard that before and was skeptical, but I asked him how.

He said: "I was a second year medical student in Vienna in 1914, but then the war started and I was drafted into the Austro-Hungarian Army, made an officer, and put in charge of a prison camp near Belgrade. I was not a very stern commandant, and I would let the prisoners' wives come to visit on Sunday.

At the end of the War, I was an Austrian officer in the wrong part of the Empire, and found myself tied to a tree. I thought this was the end of me when a group of men on horses came riding up.

One of them was a former prisoner, and he said to me, "You said you studied medicine—do you want to be our doctor? Of course, I agreed and rode with Mihailovic's partisans for about three years. After a while they decided they trusted me and sent me into port to pick up some supplies. I hopped on the first ship I could find leaving the harbor and ended up in Cleveland, Ohio."

I have heard a lot of stories since, but that was certainly one of the most unique.

———o———

Mrs. Harris was an elderly white woman who came to see me complaining of difficulty sleeping. I thought she was probably anxious and offered her a prescription for Valium,® a popular sedative of the time.

She snorted and said, "I don't want any of that junk. A doctor gave my granddaughter some, and I took them away from her and flushed them down the toilet!

Let me tell you about me. On December 7th, 1941, I was living at Pearl Harbor, where my husband was stationed, and saw the bombs dropping. I went out and commandeered a truck and was driving it around, stopping, and helping the men load the wounded on the truck so I could take them to the hospital. Col. Jones came up and said, "Mrs. Harris, you can't be out here, there is a war going on."

I told him, "I know. I can't shoot a gun, but I can drive a truck, so get the hell out of my way."

He did. I volunteered for medical service and was trained as an aide, and worked in a hospital for the duration of the war. I don't need a sedative!"

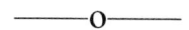

———o———

The colonel was a kindly old gentleman who was seeing me for severe hypertension. There was a new drug on the market, called Capoten® that worked differently from everything else then available, so I prescribed him some. He came back a month or so later complaining of feeling bad, so I checked some lab work and discovered that he had developed acute kidney failure. Among other things, I stopped his medications, and he got better. Since his blood pressure went back up, we restarted some of the drugs, including the Capoten®, and darned if he did not get kidney failure again. Fortunately, stopping the drug got him back to normal again. About that time a case series of similar patients was published, defining the mechanism of the phenomenon. We were able to use that information to address his problem.

One day I read an article in the local newspaper describing a reunion of the surviving members of "Doolittle's Raiders" who had bombed Tokyo early in 1942. The colonel's name was listed there. He had not mentioned this to me, so I brought it up saying: "I saw your name in the paper a few weeks ago."

He replied: "Yes, but unfortunately, so did someone else. My house was burgled while we were away."

Later I had occasion to see a museum display, which included the officers and men who took part in that flight. The colonel was one of the flight leaders, but he never said anything about it other than that one comment. I find this a striking contrast to the glib use of the term "hero" in today's media. The colonel helped lead a one-way mission designed mainly to boost morale at home, not inflict serious damage upon the Japanese empire. He did not talk about the mission or his role, because he was "just doing his job," even though it was considered remarkable even at the time it was performed. And he was fully aware that some of his men did not survive the mission.

Mr. Apple was one of those patients we dreaded to hear was being readmitted. He was a World War II veteran who had been hospitalized so many times his chart was more than two feet thick. He was known for a generally combative attitude toward "the system," which we sometimes felt as being directed at us. As the medical student, it would be our job to review all of that information and try to condense it into a couple of succinct paragraphs. One night I drew the short straw.

As part of the physical exam, I noted he had an incision in the right upper quadrant of his abdomen that was about two inches long. Nowadays, we might expect such a scar in a person who had undergone laparascopic procedure, but in those days, we only did open procedures with a large incision.

I asked him what sort of surgery he had undergone and he replied laconically, "Japanese bayonet."

It turned out he had survived the Bataan Death March and four years as a POW under unimaginable conditions. My attitude toward him underwent a major adjustment that night—continued resistance was the hallmark of his life, not something he did to aggravate young doctors.

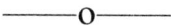

Not all the war stories were grim. The colonel was a retired Army doctor whose service included being commander of a MASH unit during the Korean war. On one clinic visit he recalled that the French Surgeon General was making a tour of Korea to see what was new in military medicine. At the time MASH units were cutting edge, so the Surgeon General came to the his hospital for a visit. While there he decided he wanted to see the front. The colonel said the Chinese were in the habit of opening their artillery bombardment at "1300 sharp."

The colonel said "I got a couple of jeeps and some of my medics as drivers, and off we went. At the time, the hospital was supporting a British Guards regiment, and when we arrived at regimental headquarters, the OIC insisted on serving tea and being sociable. I kept watching the clock and as it edged closer to 1300, I got more and more interested in heading back.

Unfortunately, we were late getting started, but the bombardment was not. We jumped out of the jeeps and I got into a foxhole with a British Tommy, who periodically directed automatic weapons fire downrange. Eventually, though, a soldier was hit, and the cry "Medic" went up. One of my medics peered over the edge of the foxhole, saw the wounded man, crawled over to him, grabbed his jacket, and pulled him into the foxhole, where he started first aid.

At this point the Tommy said: "Blimey, mate. I wouldn't want your job. It's too bloody dangerous!"

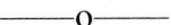

After telling my story of the month, she said: "I can tell you a true story that is even better. My father gave a ring to a girl before he shipped out for France during World War I. While he was overseas, she changed her mind, wrote him a "Dear John" letter, gave the ring to my grandmother and got married to someone else. Well, Dad came home from the War, married my Mom and raised a family. Both of them lost their spouses and after awhile, they started dating again. Eventually they decided to get married after all.

One of their friends, who knew about the "Dear John" letter, asked him one day what was different about getting married later in life, compared to earlier. Dad thought about it a moment and said: "Probably the big difference is that now, whoever gets up first has to help the other one <u>out</u> of bed."

Many of the stories were set in less dramatic circumstances, but were no less important. There was Mr. Taylor, for example, who had only gone to school through the fifth grade. He believed in education and was proud that his daughter was nationally recognized for her accomplishments as a school principal in Fayette County. Then there was Mrs. Smith, who ran the local high school cafeteria. She saw to it that all of her children obtained college degrees. One of her happiest moments was traveling to Washington, D. C., as the guest of honor of her granddaughter, who was being awarded a PhD from Georgetown.

Naturally, many of the stories revolved around the racial divide, which is particularly sharp in our part of the country. However, the division is not always quite as clear as I sometimes expected.

Mr. Williams for example, was being followed by the V. A. in Memphis for his chronic kidney disease, but set up an appointment to see me. He was an amiable African-American gentlemen, so I was surprised when he said: "I decided to come see you, because you have been taking care of Pete. And if you can get along with Pete, then you must be a good doctor." He then laughed. Since Pete was an often cantankerous white farmer, I was curious as to how they knew each other.

"Pete and I were raised together. My mama and daddy were dirt poor and didn't have anything to feed me with. They were sharecropping for Pete's father. Well, he took me in, put me to work on the farm, and fed me at his table right along with Pete. I got drafted into the Army and sent to Korea, but fortunately, it was after the war. I was not a very good soldier, but I kept my head down and did my time. When I came home I got a job at the arsenal. I never got much education, but I made sure all my kids did better than me." Pete confirmed he was almost like a brother to him. Mr. Williams was one of the mourners at Pete's funeral.

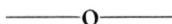

Overt racism is less commonly expressed today than was once the case, although I still have the occasional patient say something revealing their true feelings. But racism can be bi-directional.

Dr. Lucius F. Wright

I was asked to see an elderly African-American woman who had been admitted to the ICU by the UT Family Practice service. She was dying of what is called "multi-organ dysfunction syndrome," meaning that infection was overwhelming her body. Among other things her kidneys had shut down. I did not think she was going to survive, and did not think dialysis would do her any good. I was standing in the hall explaining this to her husband, who seemed overwhelmed by what was happening, but also seemed to understand what I was saying.

Unfortunately, their son, who had clearly been drinking to excess even though it was not yet noon, lashed out and said: "You're only saying that because she's black. You wouldn't say that to a white man." The father and the Family Practice resident, who was also black, were upset by his remark and wanted to apologize to me. Since I was comfortable my advice was "color-blind," I had already shunted the attack aside as a combination of grief and alcohol.

He developed paranoid schizophrenia, which got him a disability discharge from the Marine Corps. Like many such patients, he was fine as long as he took his medications, but was prone to stop taking them. The dialysis nurses had gotten pretty good at spotting early signs of breakdown in his control, and had been able to get him back on his medications. This time, though, he had started making loud, racist comments in the waiting room, causing significant distress for some of the other patients. I was asked for input on what to do. The nurses did not want to discharge him from the unit, as he had already been discharged from all of the other available places.

At that time we had another patient on his shift, who had been kicked out of his first unit because he "scared" the nurses. I interviewed him before accepting him in transfer. He was a large man and he had a loud voice, but did not strike me as particularly aggressive or hostile. It turned out he ran a bail bond business. I pointed out the dangers of using the vocal skills he used with his customers on the staff, and he promptly understood my point. In fact, he had become one of the "godfathers" of the unit, looking out for a lot of the less assertive patients.

I approached him one day on rounds about the problem with the former Marine. He indicated he was already aware of the issue.

I said: "I need you to take care of this situation, but I don't want to hear anything about it."

He said: "Yes, sir. I'll take care of it."

After that, he made a point of coming to the unit earlier than necessary and sitting in the waiting room next to the former Marine. Since he was at least twice as big as the Marine, that was all it took. The problem went away, and I never heard anything from staff or patients. I guess it illustrates the old adage about patients with mental illness: they may be crazy, but they are not stupid.

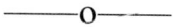

Fred was an active member of his church and also coached Little League baseball. He told me one time: "Doc, there aren't many black men who get involved with the kids. I gotta try to keep them out of trouble."

The theme of community breakdown and race relations were common topics in office visits as he struggled to overcome his depression. He got progressively more distressed by the invasion of his neighborhood by gangs of teenaged males. Sadly, during one of his last visits, he told me things had reached a new low. He said his "white teenaged grandson" had been outside when one of those gangs came by and started taunting him about his skin color. The grandson retaliated later in the day, but was arrested and put in jail. I think Fred's despair that he had not been able to protect even his own grandson led him to give up. He died shortly thereafter.

Racism is the most obvious cultural divide, but not the only one. We may have made some progress bridging the divide of racism, but we still have problems related to sexual orientation. One patient, for instance, had been in living

Stories of Life

with his same sex partner for many years. His family had ostracized him. When he died, though, there were problems, because his significant other had no legal standing, so we could not just talk to him about funeral arrangements. It seemed wrong at the time, and still does, that the only person mourning the patient's death was legally excluded.

We eventually found a brother, who lived out of state, whose response was on the order of do whatever you want. So we did what the "spouse" wanted.

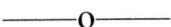

He considered himself a medical miracle as he had survived multiple transplants. His biggest worry was that he had been in a committed long-term relationship with another man, a fact which his mother simply refused to acknowledge. During previous hospitalizations, she had proven difficult to deal with.

One day he was seeing me in the office, accompanied as usual by his significant other, and said: "I think I'm about at the end of the road."

I replied: "You can't go yet. I need you to outlive your mother."

He said: "Sorry, but that is not going to happen."

Indeed, he deteriorated rapidly and ended up being hospitalized one more time. To my surprise, his mother and the significant other worked out some sort of arrangement in their shared grief and there was no special difficulty.

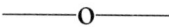

The patient was transferred from another hospital critically ill and in need of urgent dialysis. He was accompanied by his mother, a well-dressed lady in her 70's. I got her consent for treatment and asked if he had other family.

She replied: "He has been divorced for years and has no children. He does have a lady friend who lives with him, but he has never married her."

Her tone of voice suggested tension, so I asked: "Is that going to be a problem?"

She said: "If it is, you'll never know about it."

She was as good as her word. They coordinated visiting times and stayed focused on their loved one. Sadly, he did not survive the acute illness, but I appreciated the class with which they handled their interpersonal issues.

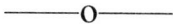

He was a "service connected" VA beneficiary, which meant he had a disability retirement from the Armed Services. He was proud of his service and told me on more than one occasion: "Doc, I've got 16 kids and I got all of them signed up for benefits."

Before he died, he told me he was up to 20 acknowledged children. Though he was not married to any of the mothers, he was proud of the fact that he gotten them all "signed up."

———o———

Over the years many of my stories revolved around situations where I was trying to help a patient whose culture that I did not understand fully or perhaps at all.

I became responsible for Sallie's dialysis when I started rounding in the unit in San Antonio. All I knew about her was that she was from East Tennessee and that her husband, an active duty soldier, had needed to come home from Korea on emergency leave to bring her back from East Tennessee after her family had held a "curing session," and taken her off dialysis.

She was usually sullen and withdrawn, but on this Monday she actually seemed cheerful. My nurse, who was from California, was making rounds with me that day. When I saw Sallie's improved mood, I said to her: "You look cheerful, today. You must have gone to church yesterday."

She replied: "Nah—didn't go to church."

I said: "You didn't? What would those snake-handling kinfolk of yours think if they knew you were backsliding?"

Fannie said: "I ain't got no snake-handling kinfolks."

I replied: "Aw, c'mon. I'm from Tennessee and I know where you're from. You can't kid me."

She grinned and said: "Well, I don't have too many snake handlers."

All the while my nurse was exclaiming: "Snake-handling? Snake-handling? What in the world are you talking about?" I explained the background for my comment to her later. I don't think she understood, but then I am not sure I do, either.

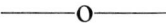

Cultural assumptions can get in the way. One of the first patients I was asked to evaluate when I started work in Denver was a Sioux Indian woman from the Pine Ridge Reservation. I had been told what her problem was, based on her evaluation prior to being evacuated to us, so I went in to "do a history and physical."

I started asking all the usual questions, but she just looked at me and said nothing. I became concerned that she did not speak English, so I went and found a senior doctor and asked him if people from the reservation spoke only their native tongue.

He replied: "Oh, they all speak English. But in their tradition, a good medicine man is supposed to figure out for himself what is wrong with you. If she has to tell you what is wrong with her, your medicine won't do her any good."

Clearly, my notion of listening long enough for the patient to tell me what was wrong was diametrically opposed to her concept of a medical encounter. Sadly, she was right—my medicine could not help her. She died later that day.

―――o―――

I had just spent several hours talking to a Hispanic family, whose loved one was brain dead, about the possibility of organ donation. Although they had seemed receptive at first, in the end they declined. This family was Catholic, and the Church had put out official statements to the effect that brain death was a legitimate basis for determining death and organ donation was appropriate for Catholics to consider. But I had the feeling there was something else going on. Since I was new to San Antonio, and had not previously had many encounters with Hispanic patients, I decided to explore things a bit more. I asked our division secretary, whose parents had been born in Mexico, if she had any insight.

She commented: "Well, I have heard the old folks say you can't get into heaven if you don't have all your parts." Official pronouncements are not powerful enough when confronting traditional beliefs.

Dr. Lucius F. Wright

———o———

Over time, I became more familiar with Hispanic traditions, and it once helped me to diagnose a patient correctly.

She had been admitted the night before and the team and I were rounding on her. The intern was "presenting" her case to the team for our input and discussion. Since this was occurring in July, I was expecting to have more input than might have been needed later in the year. She had been at her local ice-house when she experienced severe burning chest pain, mostly behind her breast-bone. It had not gone away, so she eventually went to the Emergency Room. She did not have any findings of a heart attack, but the ER doctor thought she needed to be admitted for a "work up" of the problem.

When I looked at her, I thought she was probably hypothyroid, which explained most of the chemical abnormalities concerning the team, but I also thought I knew what had caused her chest pain. I asked her what she had been eating, and she replied "peppers." Many of the poorer folk in San Antonio did not have air conditioning, so they went to their local ice-house, which as the name implies was a place that manufactured ice, but also served beer and food, and ate spicy chili peppers in an effort to break a sweat, a phenomenon we call gustatory sweating. In the relatively dry air of a San Antonio summer, this would create some evaporative cooling and relief from the heat. The hypothyroidism might also explain why she had experienced esophageal pain this time, when she had not in the past.

The house staff consulted the cardiology service, who did a workup anyway. She did not have coronary artery disease.

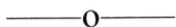

Cultural traditions also include folk wisdom regarding healing. I first ran into this with Jake, an elderly man who came to the ER with findings of heart failure. He was on no medication when I saw him, and responded quickly to the first doses of medication with relief of symptoms. I fixed him up with prescriptions and sent him home. He came back 32 days later with the same symptoms and no medications. I checked, and he had filled the prescriptions I had given him, but had not obtained the refills. He was not demented, and although illiterate, appeared to have normal intelligence. I called the social worker in for help. She was older and wiser than I, and quickly determined the cause. He operated on a theory of disease that in Western medicine is attributed to Galen.

Galen proposed that humans consisted of four humors, so disease occurred when one or more of these humors was present to excess or was lacking. The goal of the physician was to restore the proper balance of these humors. Jake assumed that the medicine I gave him was going to cure him, since it worked so well—he simply had no notion that one had to continue taking the medication to keep the "humors" in balance. A refill just "did not compute."

———o———

Reasoning by analogy is common in medical practice, but can be fallacious. About two years after the episode with Jake, I had an encounter with an elderly woman who also had heart failure. She was also poor and illiterate, so when she came back to the hospital about 10 days after discharge with recurrent symptoms and a history of non-compliance, I thought we had another "Jake."

I asked her what happened, she said: "I threw them pills under the bed."

I asked why, she said: "The Devil is under there and he needs them." She did not appear to be mentally ill and appeared to have normal intelligence, so I called the social worker again.

She came in, took one look, and said: "Do you want to go to Ketonah?" Kethonah was the county "retirement home" where indigent patients could be admitted for what is now called intermediate care. The patient said that she did and discharge arrangements were made. She was willing to take her medications—she was just trying to get someone's attention to what she really needed, which was not more pills.

Stories of Life

———o———

He was 16 when I first saw him and I knew he was going to need dialysis and a kidney transplant. His mother was absent, but his father was there and seemed to be an involved care-giver. I approached him about donating a kidney to his son and he categorically refused to even consider it. I had children that age, and did not understand his position, but did go ahead and get the patient listed for a transplant. Sadly, he got sick and died before this could be done. I still remember how upset I was when I talked to his father about his son's death.

A couple of years later I went to Australia on sabbatical. One day I attended their transplant conference, where they discussed patients who were waiting for a kidney. To my surprise, many of the patients were children, some of whom had been waiting a long time. In the US, we usually try to get the kids off dialysis as quickly as possible, and most of the time the child's mother will offer to donate. I asked my Australian hosts why their mothers weren't donating. One of them said: "The parents usually assume it is tough luck for the little kid, but they don't see the point in jeopardizing their own health. Survival of the fittest, I guess.

It reminded me of my time in the Sinai, where we tried to provide medical mission support to the indigenous Bedouin population. The Israelis, who briefed us before they left, said that the tribes would not vaccinate their kids, but they would arrange for the elders to undergo things like bypass surgery. As it was explained to us, infant mortality was a fact of life, but elders represented a store of tribal wisdom. Preservation of that wisdom, if possible, was very worthwhile.

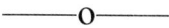

In my practice, one of the major challenges is to explain complex ideas in ways people of all degrees of education and sophistication can understand and incorporate into their decision making. This goes under the rubric of patient education. Over the years, I think I have gotten pretty good at it, but I am not always as successful as I think. I remember the older fellow I was talking to about how to take care of his wife's medical problem.

He listened to me patiently, but finally said: "Doc, I ain't gonna be able to do that. You see, I'm a simple fella. Why, I could even screw up a two car funeral."

Although I had never heard the expression before, or since, I understood he was telling me the old Army principle of "KISS"—keep it simple, stupid.

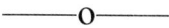

I have learned over the years that stories are one good way to get these ideas across, and use them liberally. Sometimes, though, the patient provides me with the stories that I then use to help others.

Stories of Life

He was a locally prominent citizen who came to me for evaluation. I was giving him what I call my "sermon," which deals with how to think about the difficult issues involved in pursuing dialysis treatment. I told him that it was important to have a positive reason to keep living, because fear of dying would not prove sufficient motivation to keep going when the inevitable complications arose.

He thought about that a minute and said: "Let me put it to you this way. I'm prepared, but I'm not homesick." I have used that phrase ever since.

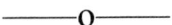

She was a middle-aged woman with obesity, diabetes, and early kidney failure. As part of her counseling, I talked to her about weight loss. I told her that I no longer discussed "diets," because they did not work. Instead I talked about "mindfulness," that is, becoming aware of what you are actually eating and why.

She responded: "Oh, I know what you are talking about. When my doctor said I needed to come see you, it frankly scared the heck out of me, because you have already taken care of Uncle Bill and Aunt Sue—I know who you are and what you do. I decided I had better get serious about my diabetes, so I decided I would start by keeping a log of everything I put in my mouth for a whole week and then go back and look at to see what I was doing wrong. When I looked back, I discovered something that horrified me.

I keep a daycare—I have 25 little kids in my house five days a week. I have gotten in the habit of giving them suckers for tea parties. They will lick on them awhile and then put them down. I discovered that I was going along behind them, picking up the suckers, and eating them. I am eating 10-12 suckers a day, and the funny thing is that I really don't care for them all that much. If someone said, "Here—have one," I would say "No, thanks," and not feel bad at all.

I have used her story ever since as an illustration of what it means to become mindful.

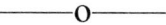

Everyone hopes to grow old, but many people seem to assume they can do this without any disability. I suppose these people hope to be like the "Deacon's One Horse Shay," simply falling apart at a ripe old age. After years of study, I have concluded, though, that there are really only two approaches to getting old—there are those people who want to wear out, and then there are those who want to rust. This basic attitude often determines how people deal not only with aging, but with disability. The following stories are examples of people with a good perspective.

He was old and frail, but his wife had Alzheimer's disease, so he decided to undergo dialysis. One night he fell at home and could not summon help from either his wife or sister, who lived with them, for several hours. When I talked to him afterward he said:

"You know I'm weak, my sister is deaf and my wife's not in her right mind. We have three people in my house, but we don't add up to one whole person."

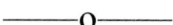

She was an elderly Italian war bride who came to see me complaining of generalized joint and muscle pain. At the time I saw her, I had just learned about fibrositis, trigger points, and local steroid injections. I injected her trigger points and she got good relief. She used to come in about once every three months or so for a "tune up." I saw her the last time just before I left when she came limping down the hall saying " ah-doctah, I needa help. I overdid in the garden pulling weeds and now I'm a dying." She got one last set of injections.

She came in for her clinic visits every three months, but twice yearly she would announce: "Give me a good tune-up. I'm going to Lost Wages next week, and I don't won't to miss any time away from the roulette wheel because I'm sick."

She was attentive to my health, too. About every six months she would bring me a fifth of Johnny Walker and encourage me to drink it. I think I may still have part of one of those bottles.

———o———

I first met Cary when he had been admitted to the hospital by one of my colleagues. When he called me about the consult he said, "This boy played in a band with one of my cousins, so he is probably doing drugs like him." It turned out Cary had a habit in addition to his diabetes and kidney failure. Over a period of a couple of years, our relationship developed to the point where he was honest about the problem and stopped trying to get me to write prescriptions. Then miracle of miracles, he got religion, got sober, and stayed that way.

Unfortunately, his diabetes progressed and he ended up on dialysis. Later we had to amputate first one leg and then the other. He actually adjusted well. He came to see me one fall afternoon and told me that he and a friend had gone to their local high school football game the previous Friday. He was proud of his new prostheses and decided he wanted to climb up into the grandstand to sit with friends. Unfortunately, the toe of one prosthesis caught in the riser and he pulled the device off. Of course he fell into the lap of the person closest to him.

Stories of Life

Any embarrassment was averted, though, when the friend said to everyone in earshot, "Dang it, Cary, I thought I told you not to lose your body parts."

Cary took to wearing shorts to show off his prostheses. One day he came by and was teasing my office nurse about the upcoming UT-Alabama football game. My nurse was from Alabama, so Cary was giving her a hard time, predicting a UT victory.

I heard him and came out of the office and said to him, "Now Cary, you know you don't have a leg to stand on."

I had forgotten a new nurse was starting her orientation that day. She heard the whole thing, but did not know the story of the football game. I still remember her look of horror at my "insensitivity."

Cary, on the other hand, laughed and said "Good one, Dr. Wright."

Alabama won the football game that year, too.

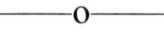

Ralph had an inflammatory bowel disease called Crohn's disease, which had destroyed much of his intestines and had given him kidney stones, and then kidney failure. One day when making dialysis rounds he stopped me and asked me: "Can I get another kidney stone now that I am on dialysis?"

Unfortunately, the answer was yes. I asked him why he had asked the question and he said he was starting to have some of the early symptoms. He said he would call me if things got worse. They did, and he showed up in the ER late the following evening with classic kidney stone pain. The X-rays showed that the stone was obstructing the flow of urine in one kidney, so I put in a request for the radiologist to put a tube into the pelvis of the kidney to relieve the pressure. Sometimes it is also possible to extract the stone this way, and I told him to go ahead and get it out if he could.

He called me back after completing the procedure and said that Ralph did not have a stone, but he was obstructed with some gummy material that he could not identify. He had sent some of it to Pathology. The pathologist made a slide and told me that it was a mass caused by an accumulation of the same fungus that gives babies diaper rash. The fungus had multiplied in his kidney to the point where it had become a "ball." Although I had not encountered this problem before, a review of the medical literature showed that it had happened to other people, and treatment with ordinary drugs usually produced a good result. I started these on Ralph and he got over this episode and did well.

About two years later I got a call in the office one afternoon from Ralph's wife. She said: "I'm in Atlanta at a business conference and Ralph is with me. He is getting the same symptoms he had when he had the fungus ball. There is absolutely no way I am going to take him to an Emergency Room here in Atlanta and tell them he has a fungus ball. They'll think I'm nuts. We are flying back to Memphis at 8 PM tonight and will be at the ER by 10."

They did and she was right, he had another fungus ball. This time I treated it without having to put him through another procedure and the problem went away again. I told him I had seen patients from Arkansas, Mississippi, and Kentucky, but this was the first time I had seen a patient from Atlanta.

———o———

When I first tell patients that dialysis and transplant are in their future, the universal reaction is some variant of "I can't possibly do that." One of the truly remarkable facts is that most people adjust, often quite quickly. I have taken to telling them to think of dialysis as a part-time job—not necessarily the best, but probably not the worst one they have ever had.

She was 19 and working full time when I first met her. Unfortunately, her kidney disease progressed and she had to start dialysis. I called the unit and got her a time for her first treatment and sent her on her way. She showed up at the appointed time, came into the unit, then panicked and ran out into the street in front of the clinic and refused to come in. The nurse spent about an hour calming her down until she was finally able to come in and get started.

She learned quickly how to take care of herself in this strange new world. Less than a year later she called me one morning and said: "My blood pressure is too low, I think they got me below my dry weight. I'm on my way to the ER in Milan to get some IV saline."

About an hour later she called me again and said: "I'm on my way back to the clinic in Humboldt. These "idiots" (not exactly the word she used) want to do lab and x-rays before the doctor sees me and won't give me the saline. Tell them I'm on the way." She got her saline and was fine.

She had been on dialysis 20 years and was serving as a patient representative to a government funded organization known as the ESRD Network. Our network includes Tennessee, Alabama, and Mississippi. The patient committee from these states was meeting in Jackson, and we were asked to arrange a program. She told her story to the group. She also pointed out that she tried to share her story with as many new patients as possible. She pointed out to each of them that she had been scared, too, but she was okay, and they would be, too.

———o———

Sometimes, events develop rapidly, giving patients and families little time for adjustment. Even then, most do eventually adapt.

The ER doctor called me to come see an acutely ill 18 man, whose blood pressure was sky high and who had severe kidney failure on his lab work. When I got there two of the ER doctors were arguing about his chest x-ray, trying to decide if he had pneumonia.

I went into the room and realized he was on the merge of a cardiac arrest, so I promptly used my "command voice" to summon more nurses and respiratory therapists. I sent his mother out to the "consultation room" to wait until I got things under control. I did get things under control and made arrangements for urgent dialysis. I then went looking for Mom.

As I walked in the room, she was talking on her cell phone. She promptly ended the call, but something I must have heard in passing made me think she already knew me. I asked: "Who else in the family have I treated?"

She replied that I had seen her father, and then told me his name. Fortunately, I remembered him and his diagnosis, which I stated to her. I then told her that her son was going to be okay, but was going to need dialysis and a transplant. Since I already had a relationship with her family, she was able to be reassured by my statements in a way that might not have been possible if I were a complete stranger.

He did do well. She donated a kidney to him, and he has subsequently complete his undergraduate degree, gotten married, and has started his family.

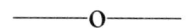

———o———

Some patients may be able to get a kidney from a family, but most get a kidney from someone who gets killed in such a way that his or her heart is still beating when they get to the hospital. We used to call this a cadaver kidney, but now we use the term "deceased donor." Both euphemisms cover the fact that every successful transplant is accompanied by someone else's tragedy. For those waiting for someone else's very bad day, the stress can be difficult.

Steve came to see me one Friday with symptoms and lab tests consistent with end stage kidney failure. I counseled him and advised admission to the hospital to start dialysis as soon as possible. I recommended we then pursue a transplant. He said: "Okay, but I can't come to the hospital until Monday. My daughter's wedding is tomorrow."

He had been on the transplant waiting list for about two years when he came to see me in the office. "Take me off the list—I'm tired of waiting." I talked him out of withdrawing, and he did get a successful transplant later that year.

Sometime afterward, we decided to organize a luncheon for patients waiting for a transplant and invited recipients to come. We also invited the newspaper, since this was during "Organ Donation Awareness" week.

When Steve was invited to tell his story he started by telling the group about his decision to come off the list. "I got disgusted with the waiting and told Dr. Wright to take me off the list. He talked me out of it, which I am glad for now. However, when the phone call finally came, I was so upset I had to go throw up before I got in my truck and drove to Memphis."

———o———

Some patients, of course, have to cope not only with their diseases, but also with the curves that life throws at them.

She was a young woman with severe hypertension. When her family doctor sent her to me, she had already suffered a stroke that left her with some disability. Over the years, her blood pressure problems led to kidney failure and she needed dialysis, and ultimately had a kidney transplant. I got to know her and her husband reasonably well. In fact, I began seeing her husband for blood pressure problems, too. Both of them admitted to stress about their son, who apparently had a drug problem and was "hanging out with a bad crowd."

She was in for a regular checkup and, unusually, her blood pressure was elevated. I had seen a short news item in the paper a few days before to the effect that her son was on trial for armed robbery. I told her I knew what she was dealing with, and that I did not want to make any change in her medications on that visit. I did not see an article about the outcome of the trial, so when she came for her next visit I asked her how it turned out.

She said: "He got 10 years at Brushy Mountain."

I asked her how she felt about it, and she said: "I didn't raise him to rob banks."

Her blood pressure was back under good control.

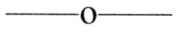

———o———

George's wife had Alzheimer's disease and he had long since put her in the nursing home. His routine was well established. He would get up, eat breakfast, tend to household chores, then go the nursing home about 10:30 to visit with her and feed her lunch. Then he would go back home. He followed the routine seven days a week for more than seven years, even though she had stopped recognizing him years ago.

He came to see me a couple of weeks after her death. He was experiencing severe bereavement, and was shocked at the behavior of the "casserole queens" who had come to call on him. I pointed out there were a lot more old women than old men.

He agreed, but said: "I think some of them have been reading the obituaries daily just waiting for their chance to make a pass at me."

We had just started a grief recovery program at the church, and I thought he would benefit. He went, and reported that it really helped. About six months later he came for a visit and when I came into the room he had a sheepish grin.

I took one look and said: "Oh, no! One of the casserole queens got you."

He said: "Not one of the queens, but yes, I have someone I want you to meet."

He then went out to the waiting room and called her in to visit. They got married shortly afterwards. She took care of him after he started dialysis, but sadly, she developed kidney failure and had to go on dialysis, too. By then, he had been dead for several years and she did not do well. I don't think her heart was in it.

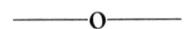

———o———

I had been seeing her for some time when her husband was referred for evaluation of kidney failure. She died abruptly and it was about six months before he came in for his next visit. He was accompanied by his new wife. Unfortunately, his kidney function had gotten worse, so I had to talk to him about dialysis. As I got started, she interrupted me and said to him: "What is he talking about? Why didn't you tell me about this? I've already buried two husbands, and I'm not ready to go through this again."

He started dialysis, but did not do well, and died shortly thereafter. She made an appointment to come see me about six months later. She was still upset and angry with him. I thought if she could "dig him up and fuss at him some more," she probably would. She never did figure out he lied to her because he did not want to die alone.

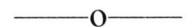

———o———

Family support is a critical factor in successful adaptation. For instance, I first saw her when the resident called me from the ER for a stat consult. When I got there I found a 13 year old girl who had severe hypertension, kidney failure, and was having seizures. Her father, who was at the bedside, told me she had just been discharged from Vanderbilt the day before, and had been discharged from LeBonheur only a few days before the admission at Vanderbilt. The residents were relieved when I told them I would put her on my service and let them follow along for educational purposes.

She actually did quite well. She had good support from her parents and her sisters. As I got to know them, though, it was clear she was a "Daddy's girl." She looked more like him than she did her mother, and was also temperamentally more like him. With his support, she got through numerous complications of her underlying disease and the attendant psychological crises. Unfortunately, he died unexpectedly from a stroke, and she was never quite the same. She lost the psychic energy to continue her struggle despite the best efforts of her mother and sisters.

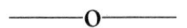

———o———

Unfortunately, not everyone is able to cope. I still remember the man who came to see me about his kidney failure, which was at a moderate stage. He asked me if dialysis was in his future and I said it was, although I thought it might be two or three years down the road. The next day I read in the newspaper where he had committed suicide. Needless to say, I spent hours going over that visit in my head, trying to figure out if it was something I said or the way that I said it which caused him to decide to give it up then and there.

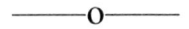

———o———

He was young and had been born with significant cerebral palsy and some mental retardation. Then he needed to start dialysis for kidney failure.

His mother, a preacher's wife, was open with me about her feeling of frustration—taking care of him had turned into her whole life, and that was not what she wanted; she was not prepared to resign herself to that life, either. Yet, as a preacher's wife, she could not express her frustration openly. She was sure her congregation would condemn her for not willingly shouldering her cross.

His blood pressure became unmanageable, and I recommended we destroy the kidneys by having the radiologist inject alcohol into them through a catheter. Although this would be painful, I thought it would be easier on him than a surgical procedure to remove his kidneys. He and his mother agreed, and the procedure was done on a Friday.

Sunday, my partner called and said that he was now paralyzed and that the CT scan showed he had spinal cord infarction, undoubtedly related to the procedure. I came back in, feeling terrible about this complication, to be met by his mother, whose frustration had reached a boiling point. She kept saying that as bad as his CP had been before, now it was worse, and he was going to be even more dependent than before. I arranged for the patient's transfer to Memphis and I still remember seeing her sitting up front in the ambulance as they drove away from the hospital. I was reasonably sure she would end up suing all of us for malpractice, but she did not.

A couple of years later, I was making a visit to Memphis and ran into the patient's father. He chatted with me amiably and told me he was now divorced and had left his pulpit. What he did not say, but I thought was evident, is that the divorce had caused his congregation to withdraw its support for his ministry. I wonder if things might have turned out differently if her congregation had been more interested in helping her carry her burden than in having her meet their expectations of how she should behave.

There have been many other instances, but I think I will let this one case suffice. Disease does not just affect the patient, but also all of his or her extended family. Sometimes in the busyness of the day, we can forget to include the family in our treatment, but this is a mistake.

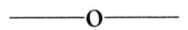

———o———

Even though I have the opportunity to get to know many of the families, there can still be surprises.

Jack had been a patient for years and I was also taking care of two brothers and a nephew from his extended family. One day he needed a ride to the hospital and we got to talking about his family. I said: "I think you must be kin to practically everybody."

He laughed and said no, not everybody. About that time the UPS truck pulled out and crossed in front of us going the other way. He waved at the driver and called him by name.

"Another cousin," he explained.

I thought I knew him fairly well, but as he was dying, one of the brothers came to sit with him and brought two young women with him. He introduced them to me as Jack's daughters. Somehow, in all those years he had never said a word about having children of his own.

———o———

The late Rev. Fred Rogers, of "Mr. Rogers' Neighborhood" fame, is quoted as saying his mother's response to a tragedy was always to say "Look around some more, because you will also see people behaving at their best."

The tornado that destroyed Mother Liberty CME Church also caused a tractor-trailer truck driving on Highland Avenue in front of the church to overturn. The driver was brought to the ER where he was found to have escaped without injury. He said that when he crawled out of the emergency hatch in the roof of his cab, he saw a bunch of people desperately trying to lift the trailer off a body trapped underneath.

The driver said it was all he could do to not laugh. "I was hauling a load of store mannequins. There was no body attached to the legs."

Nonetheless, people were trying to help any way they could.

Stories of Life

————o————

Over the years, the social workers at the Dialysis Clinic have maintained a small fund to help patients with needs not covered by the usual social service agencies. The money is raised by the patients themselves. The patients in the unit located in Brownsville, which is more economically distressed than the other locations, always raised the most money. Maybe they appreciated the idea that the "widow's mite" could matter in ways that did not seem credible to those who were better off.

————o————

I usually get a look of disbelief when I tell people I have been quoted in *The National Enquirer* twice in my career, since it is one of those publications with lurid headlines sold at the checkout stands in the grocery store. Most folks think I am setting up another one of my stories, but it is actually true.

The first episode occurred in 1993. I was busy doing a procedure in the hospital dialysis unit one morning, when I got a page from the Emergency Room. One of my transplant patients was there complaining of abdominal pain and vaginal bleeding. Even though I knew she was well into her forties, I reflexively ordered a pregnancy test along with other lab work. By the time I arrived in the ER, the pregnancy test was back and was positive.

A quick history and physical confirmed she was in labor, even though neither of us had known she was pregnant. I called the obstetricians and they promptly took her off the labor and delivery.

Her husband had not been too concerned when he brought her in, so he had gone on to his office. I called him there and the first thing I told him to do was to sit down. I then told him he was about to become a father, but not to have a car wreck on the way back to the hospital. The baby girl is now completing college and planning to go into healthcare.

They told the story to their friends and it was picked up by *The Jackson Sun*, and by *The National Enquirer* from there. A stringer called and asked for a quotation about pregnancy in patients with kidney transplants, which was accurately reported in the final story.

The second episode occurred in September 1994. Mary donated a kidney to her husband. This was one of the first non-related living donor kidney transplants done in our area, and the story made the newspaper. The same stringer called asking about the odds of this sort of thing happening. In the published version, I was quoted accurately yet again.

He died of cancer some years later and I went to the visitation at the funeral home to talk to Mary. Prominently displayed was a copy of *The National Enquirer* with the story. She said it had caused quite a stir, because her son-in-law, who was not around when this all occurred, did not know about it. He thought she was kidding, so she had to show him the proof, too.

I am still waiting for my third appearance in the pages of this tabloid.

Chapter 2

End of Life Stories

One of our great unresolved issues in medicine is end of life care. While there are many levels to understanding this problem, one factor is the nature of human experience. My father, who was a young lieutenant in combat in 1944, said he didn't think he would make 23, and was amazed to find himself still alive in his nineties.

He said: "The interesting thing about getting really old is that you look out on the world with the same eyes everyday, and the view from inside never changes. Some days I get up and look at that old man in the mirror who needs a shave, and wonder who it is. By 10:30, I've usually remembered."

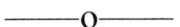

———o———

When I did a sabbatical in Australia in 1993, one of the questions I wanted to explore was why they had so few very elderly patients on dialysis. The median age of my dialysis patient population then was about 64 years old. In Australia, very few patients over 75 were on dialysis at all. When I asked the physicians there about "rationing," they all replied that the subject just did not come up all that often.

Older patients simply did not look for that sort of heroic therapy.

This led me to the question: When do patients begin to decide they are too old for an aggressive therapy?" When I asked the question in Australia, the answer was "70." When I got home and started asking the question of colleagues around the country, the consensus was "80." Some of my younger colleagues could not recall ever having a patient refuse therapy.

Combining the fact "the view from inside never changes" with a societal definition of old age that does not begin until age 80, if then, creates a perfect storm for problems.

———o———

Of course, physicians, being human, are part of the problem, too. We are often afraid to bring up the subject of death and all of us have stories about pathological family members who insist on "doing everything" long after that has stopped being reasonable. However, most stories don't have to end this way.

Faith had been seeing me for several years, and she was not bashful in telling me her story. She and her first husband had eight young children when he was killed in a car wreck. She had met Phil, who not only took her on, but the eight kids and helped raise them as his own. An ardent member of her church, she often cited Phil as proof that miracles still occured.

One day she came to see me and admitted she was starting to feel bad. I told her it was time to go ahead and get her peritoneal dialysis catheter placed and plan to start dialysis. Insertion of the catheter is done by the surgeons on an outpatient basis, so I usually don't see patients the day of the procedure. Faith happened to be in a room next to another patient that I came to see, so I popped in to say hello.

She introduced me to the daughter who was sitting there with her and said: "I'm mad at you."

I asked why and she said: "Because it is safer to be mad at you than at God. I really don't want to do this."

I told her I understood, but did not think this was good theology.

Faith lived another eight years on dialysis and when she died, Phil sent a wonderful thank you note to the nurses. In it he told of some of the good times they had experienced together in those years of treatment. He also expressed his appreciation for the care and concern they had shown to her during all those years.

We had our annual staff meeting shortly thereafter and I read his letter to the group. I told them: "I don't know about you, but that is my definition of success."

Stories of Life

―――o―――

He was about my age and a busy contractor. I had seen him a couple of times and we had discussed the fact that dialysis was in his future. He was back for a regular office visit. I asked him if he had been to see his primary care physician since our last visit, and he said he had.

He then added: "I told him I had another visit with my psychiatrist nephrologist in a couple of weeks. He gave me a funny look, so I explained—first he tells you a joke, then tells you that you are going to die, then he tells you another joke."

―――o―――

When I came into the room to start the consultation, I noticed she had a book entitled "Holy Humor" sitting on the table. I commented that it was a title after my own heart and she said: "I hope so. I am best friends with your long-term patient, Mary Simpson, and she said I should bring it to you."

―――o―――

The patient and her daughter came to see me for a consultation. Although I did not know the patient, I had met her daughter socially on a number of occasions. I evaluated Mom's condition and gave them my standard "sermon" about the issues of dialysis and end of life care.

After a number of admissions to the hospital for heart failure, it looked to me like Mom had reached the end of the road. I called her daughter out into the hall and suggested sending them home with hospice.

She said, "When Mom and I came to see you the first time, we were really upset that you talked to us about dying. She kept asking "Can he talk to us like that." Now I see why you did that. But I don't know if I can do this or not."

I talked to her some more, and told her she would have a lot of help. They did go home with hospice. Mom lived another week, during which time all of her friends and family came to tell her goodbye. The daughter told me later that she treasured the memory of that week.

She said, "I didn't think I could do it, but I am so glad you convinced me I could."

A couple of years later I ran into her coming out of the ICU. I had heard through the social grapevine that Dad was in the hospital and not doing well. I asked her how she was doing.

She said, "Oh, we know what to do this time. We had a good teacher. We have already made it clear we just want him to be as comfortable as possible."

———o———

Mr. Washington was one of the first patients in my practice after I came to Jackson. Although I did not know it at first, he was well known in town as he worked at with the public during the day and as a bartender at society parties on the weekends.

One Saturday morning, he came to the Dialysis Clinic and had a clotted access, which required that he go to the hospital for de-clotting in the Operating Room. His wife had left to go to the mall, and this was in the days before cell phones, so I picked him up at the Clinic and drove him to the hospital.

As we neared the stop sign that marked the intersection of Country Club Lane and the US 45 Bypass, he suddenly rolled the window down, leaned his head out the window, and shouted to the woman in the oncoming car, "You aren't getting me yet!"

Since I was new in town, I had not recognized the other driver and asked him who it was.

He replied, "Shirlene Mercer, with Mercer Brothers Funeral Home. But I am going with Stephenson-Shaw anyway."

I also told this story to his wife and family the night of his death some 10 years later. They had a good laugh, and then his wife said, "He's right. We want you to call Stephenson-Shaw."

She was one of those patients we thought had more lives than a cat. She had numerous admissions to the hospital for problems directly related to her unwillingness or inability to adhere to the medical regimen demanded by life on dialysis.

She was also one of those patients who was so well known in the Emergency Department that all of the staff knew and called her by her first name. She had a problem with drug abuse in addition to all of her medical problems, but I thought she came to the hospital so often because she had no one else to talk to. She decided she liked me, though, and made a very clear distinction between those social trips and the ones for real problems related to her ailments. On the social events she would tell the nurses: "Don't call Dr. Wright. The ER doctor can handle this."

In due course, she got admitted to the hospital and did not rally. She died one Friday evening. As usual, there was no one in attendance. Her only known relative was a son, who had died sometime earlier, so we ended up sending her body to the hospital morgue. It looked like she was headed to "Potter's Field."

This was in the days before the Internet, and I am not sure she would have been on the grid, even in today's world. Through heroic efforts on the part of someone in the morgue and in the police department, contact was finally made with a cousin in Missouri, who agreed she would come and see to a funeral. Since they did not have much money, either, a deal was struck with the funeral director. He charged the minimum fee and the cousin's son dug the grave so another person would not have to be paid.

———o———

He had spent his life operating a store in Selmer, Tennessee. After retirement, he wrote a memoir of his life and times and published it. He gave me a copy, which I read. There were a lot of pictures from a bygone era, but the last pictures in the book were of he and his wife, each kneeling by their tombstone, which had already been set in place.

I saw him in the office for some seven years before he finally got to a point where dialysis was needed. He did not do very well on dialysis and died in the hospital after yet another complication. As I came into the room to "pronounce him," that is to make an official declaration of death. She was there waiting for me. I asked if she was okay. She said to me: "He's finally getting to start the first chapter in his new book. I'll be okay."

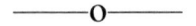

———o———

I saw Cissy's daughter, Ella, in the office and recommended a course of action, but Ella wanted to delay it to go to her high school graduation. Ella showed up in the ER three weeks later catastrophically ill. When I got to the

ER, Cissy was literally hanging unto the nurse's arm and screaming at her to save her daughter. I physically removed her from the nurse's arm and made her sit in a chair in the corner so the nurse could do her job.

Ella ended up on dialysis and I set up an office visit to talk to them in more detail about a transplant. After awhile, with an obviously pre-arranged signal, Ella got up and left the office while Cissy moved into the patient's chair.

She had two issues she wanted to discuss. First, she wanted me to know she had to be the donor, since she was not sure her husband was the biological father. She had not discussed her concerns with her husband, and did not think he had any suspicion that he might not be Ella's father. After this confession, she started crying and said:

"I just wish everything would get back to the way it was. I was happy, driving around town in my little red sports car without a care in the world. Now all I can do is worry." I pointed out that nothing would erase the memories of the traumatic events of the past 12 months, and that you "can't go home again."

She did donate a kidney to Ella, but there were continued issues that required frequent trips to see the transplant team. Sadly, on the way home from one of these, Cissy lost control of her car and suffered severe traumatic brain injury from which she never recovered. I don't know whether she ever had an honest conversation with her husband or not.

———o———

He was about 85 when I first met him. He had end-stage kidney disease and was going to need dialysis to live much longer. He did not hesitate, saying he had a lot to do and, if fact, stayed active up until about six months before his death at age 95.

One day, I was making rounds at his dialysis unit when he came in with a clotted access. He did not have a ride, did not want to use the ambulance, and the bus was not available, so I invited him to join me, since I was on my way back to the hospital anyway.

As we were riding down the highway he suddenly turned to me and said: "You know doc, I was 45 years old before I figured out a man had to die of something."

I always thought the reason he died was that he had taken a trip to visit his 106 year old sister, and she had not recognized him. That experience so depressed him that he simply gave up.

———o———

People certainly do give up. I remember an elderly woman who did well on dialysis for a couple of years until she fell and broke her hip. She got through the repair operation and the rehabilitation and seemed to be doing reasonably well from my perspective when she fell and broke the other hip. I got the surgeons to repair that one as well. I came into see her on morning rounds a few days after the second surgery and she said to me: "Doctor, I'm tired."

"Did you sleep badly last night?" I asked.

"No," she said. "I slept fine. I'm just tired."

"Tired of being in the hospital?" I persisted.

"No. I'm tired of being anywhere—just sick and tired of being sick and tired."

"Have you talked to your family," I asked.

"No, I am going to tell them when they come in this afternoon, but it is my decision and my mind is made up."

I arranged for her to go into hospice the next morning.

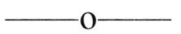

———o———

He was in his eighties and had said he did not want dialysis. One night in December he came to the Emergency Room in distress with a new heart attack and heart failure. The cardiologist and I talked to his wife about how aggressive to be, given his wishes. We also told her we did not think he would survive and that he should be "DNR." She grabbed my arm and said: "Save my husband—save him!"

I put him on dialysis to deal with the heart failure, but he did not rally and died about a month later after a long and difficult course.

Just about a year later, I got a hand addressed, bulky letter in the mail. When I opened the letter and read it, I realized it was from the wife. She wanted to know why I had "tortured her husband" with dialysis when he had not wanted it. She sent me letters every year at Christmas for the rest of her life, but I did not open any of the others.

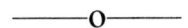

———o———

She had been an Army wife, moving from place to place as her husband pursued his career. He was quite successful and had just retired as Sergeant-Major. She had been on dialysis awhile before they retired to this area, and she had started having complications from her disease. Eventually it got to the point where she decided she did not want any further therapy, although she did want to continue dialysis. Her husband had been present for these conversations and had been supportive.

One Thursday she was so miserable I offered her hospitalization for symptomatic relief. She was reluctant, but agreed she wanted relief. She reiterated she did not want any heroics. Saturday morning about 6:30 AM, the nurses called me from the ward in a panic that she was on the verge of respiratory arrest and he was in the hall in full command mode insisting that something be done.

I figured with his background and experience there was no way the nurses were going to be able to deal with him and we might not have the ten minutes it would take for me to get there. I told them to go ahead and intubate her and start breathing for her. When I got there, she was stable enough for me to transfer her to the ICU. I then went looking for the Sergeant Major.

He was mourning and said to me several times: "I've been in four wars. It was supposed to be me that went first." I took him to the bedside, where he looked at her on the respirator and said: "God, what have I done?"

I told him: "I'm going to say to you what you have said to many young second lieutenants—I will see to it. Go home." He did and I did.

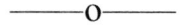

———o———

Mr. Jones had a bad heart and kidney failure, but was sent to me for consideration of dialysis. After candid discussion he said: "I'm ready to go, but my wife is dead and our son has Down Syndrome, so I feel like I have to keep on as long as I can." Unfortunately, he started having chest pain on dialysis that was so severe we had to cut the treatment short of our goal. Nothing I did medically seemed to help.

I admitted him to the hospital, got the cardiologist to evaluate him, and he recommended bypass surgery. Mr. Jones agreed to this, using the same logic he had used before. I talked to him before the surgery, because I had a foreboding and asked him about his son. He said: "Don't worry about him. I have made a plan with my church. When I die, my money goes into a trust fund, and the church has agreed to look after him for the rest of his life."

Mr. Jones had severe complications during surgery, as feared, and did not wake up afterwards. His pastor showed up at the bedside and assured me that he had the son in his care and all was well. He also said it would be okay to let Mr. Jones go without further trauma. So we did.

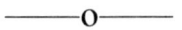

———o———

Judy was a sweet, grandmotherly sort of person who had been on dialysis a couple of years. Her husband, Joe, on the other hand was a different story. He sat in the hallway while she had her dialysis treatment and generally glowered at the world. The year before, she had gotten sick and he had lost his temper and put his hand through the wall. We all worried about what would happen when Judy died.

Judy developed an infection that would not clear, and it became obvious that her time was drawing near. I came to work that morning and was told that Judy's daughter had arrived from California and wanted to meet with me. I had her come to see me in the office expecting she wanted an update on her mother's condition.

Instead, she said: "I am here to take care of my father. You don't need to worry about him. You see, my mother abused me and my siblings while we were children. I have been in therapy about this for years, and I'm okay. But you won't be surprised that I am not going to mourn for my mother."

My children were young and I could only imagine the difficulty Joe had knowing that he was going to be deployed from time to time and while he was away, his children were going to be abused and he could not stop it. He also realized that if he filed for divorce, he would have difficulty proving she was unfit, and the odds were that she would get sole custody, given the attitudes of the time. I also realized that we had read the situation completely backward—Judy, not Joe, was the one we should have feared.

———o———

She had juvenile onset diabetes and had developed blindness and kidney failure. She fared reasonably well for awhile, but then started developing gangrene of one leg, then the other. We did several operations and she ended with above the knee amputations. She then developed gangrene in her hand and had it amputated. Through it all she never complained, and her family continued to bring her in faithfully

Stories of Life

for her dialysis. Now she was developing gangrene in her remaining hand, and I really did not want to put her through any more surgery.

I talked to her sister, who was then the primary caregiver, and expressed my misgivings. "I really don't know how she has made it this far, to tell you the truth."

She replied: "I think she is just waiting for you to tell her its okay to die."

I did and she did.

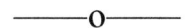

———o———

Robert started getting to where he would pass out every time he stood up. After awhile, nothing I was doing seem to help. I had just sent him home from the hospital once again when Ann came to see me in the office and asked me what to expect. I confirmed that I was out of "tricks" to improve the situation and the choices were either to keep on doing what we were doing until he died, or to stop and go with hospice. She said she did not think she could discuss it with him and would I please come out to the house and talk to him and tell him what I had just told her?

When I got to the house, Robert was in bed with his mother, adult daughter and wife waiting for me. His adolescent son was in the other room. After discussing the options with him, he said: "I wish it was that easy. I will let you know in the morning."

I assured him there was no timetable and left, knowing I had given him my permission to die, and so had his wife, mother, and daughter. Ann called me about 7 AM the next morning and told me Robert had died about 2AM, but she had waited to call, because she had not wanted to wake me up.

———o———

His wife was dying and he came to see me in the office. He was clearly grief stricken and I could not seem to find words of comfort for him. I finally asked him if he had a religious belief, and could I call a chaplain for him?

He said: "I wish I could. I call myself a Christian believer, but I have done some really bad things while I was on active duty, and I don't think I can be forgiven for them." He went on to indicate that he had been one of those people our government employs to commit assassinations, torture and other deeds in the name of national security.

All I could think of to say sounded terribly theological in my mind—a discussion of Salvation by Grace does not cut it in this kind of situation. So I said nothing at all. I have always regretted my silence, and perhaps my own unwillingness to be present with him in his moment of real repentance. I vowed to "plan ahead" so I would not be caught tongue-tied again. With experience, I came to realize that I actually had not needed to say anything—just listening was likely sufficient.

———o———

I had a chance to put these lessons into practice in an unusual situation many years later. I was flying back from Washington to Memphis after a short meeting. At first I thought the middle seat might be empty, but at the last minute a fellow a few years older than me sat down and peered anxiously out the window at the baggage conveyor belt, trying to see if his bags had made the transfer.

We exchanged the usual pleasantries and I asked him if he lived in Memphis.

"No, I live near Jackson, Mississippi, at least for now, but I am probably going to move. You see, my son died in an automobile accident six years ago and I just can't seem to get past it. My wife wants to "move on," but I can't do it."

I asked him if he had a church and he did, but said it was one of those churches where the emphasis was on happiness, even when people were not happy.

He said: "They're always saying God is good. All the time God is good. But if He is so good, why did my son die in that stupid accident?"

Having learned my lesson, I did not try to answer the question, but I did not shut him down, either. He proceeded to tell me the rest of his story, which included the fact that his elderly parents, who lived in Georgia, had been murdered in their beds and had their house set on fire to burn their bodies and hide the crime. No one had been arrested for their murders. He seemed to be suffering trials worthy of Job.

As we were getting ready to get off the plane, I told him I hoped he found what he was looking for, and he thanked me. But I got the strangest look from the woman who had been sitting in the seat in front of me—I don't know whether she was overwhelmed by the sadness of the story or thought I was an idiot for letting him tell it to me. My primary thought was it was a shame he belonged to a church unwilling to deal with the darkness and pain people suffer in this life.

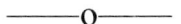

———o———

He was a Russian Jewish émigré engineer who had become despondent and taken a .22 caliber pistol and shot himself in the head. He was brought to the ER, where it was clear that he was not going to survive. I was called to see if we could get consent to "harvest" his kidneys for transplant into other patients.

His parents, wife, and two small children were all at the hospital. The father wanted to see the X-rays that showed the bullet in the brain. He moaned, grabbed his head and walked around without being able to say anything. His wife was sitting in a corner crying inconsolably. The kids were running up and down the hall yelling and screaming with no adult attendance.

His wife wanted to discuss organ donation with their rabbi, but it was a Friday evening, he was Orthodox, and they knew he would not answer the telephone. Eventually members of the synagogue showed up and offered whatever help they could. One volunteered to go to the rabbi's house and drive him back to the hospital, since he would not drive on Shabboth. Another took the kids in tow and finally got them out of the hospital.

When the rabbi arrived, he explained there was nothing in scripture, the Talmud, or tradition that prohibited organ donation. However, he clearly saw his role as that of legal scholar, not pastor, which surprised me. All I could think about was this family, who were trying to cope in the midst of a personal tragedy in a foreign country, surrounded by people who did not speak their language, and who did not understand their customs and religious traditions. And here I was asking them to make a decision in the name of unknown others for an altruistic gift of life. In the end, they gave consent, but I was never sure if their gift offered any solace in the midst of such isolation.

———o———

He had juvenile rheumatoid arthritis. By the time I met him, he was able to get around with difficulty, so he spent a lot of time at working from home via computer, something that was fairly new at the time. His wife was supportive, but worked outside the home so they could have insurance. When it came time to start dialysis, there was no question that we would pursue a home-based therapy, since travel was a challenge.

He did well on dialysis, but over time, his physical debility progressed, he started having bone fractures, and needed a great deal of pain medication to keep him comfortable. I did what I could to minimize the number of visits, kept his prescription for pain medications renewed, and kept in touch by phone. This went on for more than a year.

Then one day she brought him to the ER because he had developed fever and confusion. He had a tube placed in his airway in the ER and a respirator was attached to it. We had long since reached an understanding that he did not want heroics, including ventilator therapy, but I suggested we give the antibiotics a little while to work. It was soon apparent that they were not going to turn the tide.

She came to me and said: "I want to go ahead and take him off the ventilator now.

He always worried about me being a young widow, and I think that is why he has hung on so long. But I don't want him to suffer. But I do want the family to be here when he goes."

The staff were able to arrange for family, pastor and friends to come. They sang hymns and prayed for the six hours it took for him to die.

———o———

She was a young woman with juvenile diabetes and had a young daughter when I first met her. Unfortunately, she had also developed advanced chronic renal failure and was going to need dialysis and a kidney transplant in the near future. She asked me what her prognosis was and I gave her a less than specific answer. She challenged me and said she needed to know the facts. I told her without a transplant, the average survival on dialysis for her would be about three years.

She said "That won't do. I have a daughter I need to raise."

Over time she did need to start dialysis, and shortly thereafter her mother gave her a kidney. The transplant was successful, although she continued to have many complications. Consequently, we had many visits in the office, ER, and hospital. My kids were a little older than her daughter, so sometimes she would ask what to expect next, and we would compare notes on how to survive the teenage years and so forth.

As it happened, on her final admission I was out of town, but had come back and was on call that Monday when she had a cardiac arrest. Although we resuscitated her, she was not doing well, so I talked to her husband, and he agreed we should not do anything further.

He said he had only one request. At that point he looked at their now grown daughter, who said "If you don't, I'll ask him." He then asked me to speak at her funeral, which I agreed to do.

I looked through the chart and in the nearly 20 years I had attended her, she had been admitted to the hospital something like 42 times with various complications, yet she always managed to be grateful that my original prognosis had been wrong.

The United Methodist Church, where her husband was the pastor, placed a memorial window, a stained glass representation of a dove, over the door from the narthex into the sanctuary in her memory. As far as I know, it is still there today.

———o———

She was dying and had been in coma for days. One morning the daughter asked me to let her know when her mother's time was imminent, as they had a large family. I said I would.

A couple of days later, the nurse manager paged me and said: "She looks like she will die in the next hour. Better tell the daughter to make the calls."

She was still living when I went home that evening and, in fact, was still there the next morning. The nurse manager came up and said: "You won't believe what happened. About midnight she woke up and saw about 50 people standing around in the room talking in low voices and said—You're all here, you must think I'm dying."

She stayed up and visited with them the rest of the night, before lapsing back into coma and dying three days later. At the time I felt bad about it, but now I feel good about it—she got to tell everyone goodbye.

But I have never again let myself be trapped into trying to predict a precise time—even doctors can't know that.

Chapter 3

Doctors and Nurses

Medical practice is not, thank God, always grim. Humor abounds if you have an eye for it. Medicine is also not practiced in isolation. There are always other doctors, nurses, and literally hundreds of other persons involved in the care of every patient. It is these stories that I want to tell in this chapter.

———o———

I had been seeing John in the office for several months, and had placed a fistula in his arm anticipating the need for dialysis. He had several siblings who were potential kidney donors, so we set up a family conference. After the conference he told me he was not feeling good. After evaluating him, I decided it was time to go ahead and start dialysis. I sent him over to the Dialysis Clinic, but they could not get the needles into his fistula, so he to be admitted to the hospital to place temporary catheters into the vein in his groin.

As I was loading up a syringe with lidocaine, numbing medicine, he looked up at me and said: "I didn't know you did anything like this."

I asked him what he thought I did and he replied, "All you've ever done for me before is talk."

Patients and insurance companies don't always value "just talk" although a lot of money could be saved if people could take the time to do more of it.

———o———

The young man was a U. S. Army soldier who came from the Philippines. He needed a biopsy of his kidney, so I started counseling with him about the procedure. His command of English was weak and I soon got the impression he did not understand me. Since I had plenty of Hispanic nurses, I asked one of them to talk to him in Spanish, but it turned out their accents were so different they could not understand each other. In desperation, I put out the word to find someone who spoke Tagalog.

The librarian responded. Although she was from the Philippines, she did not speak Tagalog, but was willing to give it a try. When she got to the bedside, she and the soldier immediately started conversing in what I took to be their native tongue. It turned out they were from the same ethnic group and had no problems at all talking to each other. She asked me what I wanted him to know. I told her and she started talking to him in their unfamiliar language, gradually switched over to Spanish, then she ended up telling him about the procedure in English!

When she finished, I said to her: "Thanks, but I could have told him in English, but I did not think he spoke much English."

She replied: "He speaks English, but he learned it from the Spanish-speaking nuns at the convent school. He did not understand your accent."

———o———

She was very old and very sick, delirious and not able to swallow, so we decided to place a tube through her nose and into her stomach to give her medication and food. Now the tube is soft, so as not to injure anything, and as I tried to push it down the back of her throat, the tube kept curling up and pushing out of her open mouth instead of going down into her stomach.

In frustration I stuck my finger into her mouth and tried to push the tube the right way, but was interrupted by the patient clamping down on my finger with her teeth. I could not get her to let go, although she did not bite hard enough to cause real injury.

The medical student finally thumped her on the arm and her mouth slowly opened up. He said: "Golly, I didn't think she was going to let go until it thundered."

I have never stuck my finger into the mouth of an unconscious patient again without a bite block in place.

He had served in the cavalry before World War II and loved horses, so he rented a horse at the public park and went for a ride. Unfortunately, he fell off one day, fracturing his arm, and was brought to the hospital. While there he developed kidney failure and had to start dialysis.

He was one of those patients who wanted to be active, and the fatigue he experienced because of his anemia really bothered him. At the time, the drug we used was a male hormone known by the trade name of Deca-Durabolin.® The drug has since attained some infamy for its use in sports doping scandals. The old cavalryman got a modest response in terms of an improved hemoglobin.

One morning, after about six months of therapy, he came into the dialysis unit and announced: "I figured out what was wrong with me. I was all stopped up."

At first, we thought he was telling us that he had corrected his constipation, a common problem in dialysis patients. Our misapprehension was corrected when I got a call later that morning from his wife.

She practically screamed: "Do you know what he did? We haven't done that in 25 years. You have to take him off that medicine!" We did.

Although doctors order dialysis, nurses do the actual procedure so dialysis patients end up spending a lot of time in the hospital, where they have contact with even more nurses. These people become a very important part of the patient's life, too.

He had been born with abnormalities to his bladder and rectum. As a result, he had to undergo construction of both an ileostomy and colostomy at a young age. Due to problems with maintaining cleanliness, he ended up requiring amputation of both legs above the knees. Then he ended up on dialysis.

His family did not seem particularly involved in his care. Sanitation was still an issue, so they often brought him to dialysis in the back of their pickup truck. He had no friends that we ever saw. He did not have very good social skills and the staff did not warm up to him very much.

This went on for about five years, and he developed most of the complications one might expect. His final hospitalization began one day in mid-December and he was still there Christmas day. The hospital nurses realized no one was going to come visit him, much less bring him a gift, so they got together and bought him some clean clothes and gave him an old guitar, having found out he could play one fairly well.

I remember rounding on him that Christmas day and seeing the look of happiness on his face. I also realized that the hospital staff came closer to being family than anything he had ever experienced. He died about a month later.

———o———

Good nurses can be a big help in diagnosing obscure problems as illustrated by the patient I saw for the cardiologist. The patient had been admitted several days earlier for a procedure and the cardiologist was consulted for evaluation of unexplained tachycardia, (fast heart rate.) He had no explanation and called me in for a "second opinion."

I looked through the chart and had formulated a couple of vague hypotheses, otherwise know as guesses, but stopped to talk to the nurse before I went to the bedside.

She said: "You know, it's interesting. He gets these episodes about every four hours regular as clockwork."

I rechecked the chart and confirmed that he was getting one of his home medications, designed to prevent hyperthyroidism, every six hours. A quick check with the pharmacist confirmed the drug had a half life of about three hours—it was wearing off about hour four. The nurse solved the problem, although I got the credit.

———o———

Dietitians play an important role in dialysis care, since patients need to be very careful with what they eat if they are to get a good result. I always like to tell them of an encounter with a perky, young dietitian many years ago.

We were making rounds in a semi-private room, meaning there were two men in the same room. Nowadays that is virtually unheard of, but was something of a luxury in this particular hospital, which still had 16 man wards. Our patient was next to the window. The other patient, next to the door, had suffered from cancer of the vocal cords and had undergone laryngectomy, removal of his voice box. He had his breakfast tray sitting on the table in front of him.

The dietitian bounced into the room and said: "Good morning, Mr. Jones. How was breakfast?"

Of course, he could not talk, so he simply reached down, picked up the mass of scrambled eggs on his plate by a corner, and held them up in the air, suspended by that corner. She deflated and left the room. I never saw her again, and suspect she moved into another line of work.

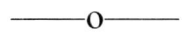

———o———

I don't take care of these patients alone. I have many doctors that I call upon to help me take care of their needs, and, in turn, I am called upon to help them with their patients.

The resident called me about noon reporting she had a patient in the ER with an intractable "metabolic acidosis," meaning a life-threatening build up of acid in his body. He was not very responsive and she thought he was dying. I asked if he was alcoholic, and she said he was. I then suggested he was probably poisoned with methanol (wood alcohol) and she needed to start an infusion of ethanol (grain alcohol) while I came in to see him and arrange dialysis. When I got to the ER, the resident had read up on methanol poisoning and realized he was a "typical case."

I still remember her comment: "You know, it is really hard to think about a diagnosis when you've never seen someone with it before."

———o———

She went into labor one evening when I was not on call. My partner called me at 6:00 AM and said, "She is in labor, needs a C-section, and won't sign the consent. You need to come in."

When I got there, my young OB-GYN associate was almost hopping from one foot to the other and there were three nurses talking to her, but she was sitting there on the bed with her arms crossed. I looked at her; she looked at me.

I said: "We've worked hard to get to this point to have a healthy baby. We need to let him do what he needs to do."

She said "Okay," and signed the consent and off they went.

The young obstetrician was very upset and frustrated, wanting to know what he had done wrong. The answer was nothing. I attended her for more than five years before she would say more than "yes" or "no."

These days she is having a contest with me to see who has the most grandchildren. Sadly, very few physicians have that kind of long-term relationship anymore. Both doctors and patients want quick results.

———o———

She was a transplant patient and became pregnant. She was followed closely by the obstetricians, who called me and told me early on they thought she was going to need a C-section. When the time came, they admitted her to the hospital and called me to see her with the note they were going to go to surgery in the morning. As I walked into the OB area, I ran into one of the obstetricians and said: "Remember, she has a pelvic kidney."

He looked startled, but said: "Thanks, but I'm not going to do her case unless she gets into trouble. It will be the on-call doctor tomorrow."

I decided on an ounce of prevention. I went to the nurse's station and got an indelible ink marker from them. I then talked to the patient and told her I wanted to mark the kidney, but I wanted her to be sure and remind the obstetrician when he came by in the morning before surgery. She agreed, and I marked the kidney, and but a big "Don't cut here" label on it.

After the baby was delivered the next morning, the obstetrician told me what happened. He had gone in to see her before going to the OR and she said: "I have a message from Dr. Wright."

He said: "I know, he left me a message in the chart."

She said: "No, he left you a message with me."

She pulled her gown up and showed him my "artwork." He said he would take all the help he could get, but we had a good laugh about it.

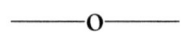

———o———

Not all memorable encounters require long-term relationships, though.

Dr. Lucius F. Wright

She was a relatively young woman who had been living in West Texas when she got sick and was hospitalized. She was trying to come home to Carroll County, but felt so bad she stopped in the Emergency Room in Jackson and was admitted to the hospital. Since her kidney function was abnormal, I was asked to see her.

One morning she said to me: "I think my kinfolks are trying to poison me."

It was possible that her kidney disease was the result of poisoning, but I really did not have any evidence and did not know what to do. One of the older doctors suggested I call Dr. Ballard, who was Medical Examiner as well as a general practitioner. He recommended I call the sheriff in Carroll County and let him know what she said, as well as the fact that I did not have proof.

I called the sheriff's office, identified myself and asked to speak to the sheriff. He came on the line and I told him the patient's name, where she lived, and what she said to me.

He asked: "Where did you say she lived again?"

I told him and he said: "Oh, them. I know that bunch. Could be. I'll send a deputy out there to check up on it. Thanks for calling."

I told this story to another sheriff and he agreed that every county or local law enforcement officer has people like this family—folks they suspect of doing bad things, even though they may not have evidence to stand up in court.

———o———

When I came into the unit, Tammy was practically yelling at the patient. I intervened and asked her what was wrong.

She said: "I told him if he didn't stop doing what he was doing, he was going to kill himself."

I told her to take a break and we would talk about it later, which we did.

I asked: "What was Alvin doing before he got sick and started dialysis?"

She was not sure, so I said: "He was working as a casual laborer—working when he needed the money. He never had a steady job, and as a result does not even have enough earned income credits to qualify for Medicare coverage. For him, a good week was one where he had enough money to eat, buy alcohol, and maybe buy the company of a woman. Now he is on dialysis and does not feel well enough to do the sort of physical work he used to do. He is not supposed to drink a lot of fluids, particularly alcohol, and has erectile dysfunction. Can you see why he isn't very interested in working to prolong his life on dialysis?"

She quit and went to work at the hospital shortly thereafter. Unfortunately, she was too young to understand that not everyone shares our attitudes toward life and death. Our patient was not suicidal, but he was also not very motivated to make difficult changes in his daily routine just to put off dying a while longer.

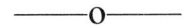

———o———

I was in my second year of medical school, when my grandmother called and asked me what I knew about cholesterol. The "cholesterol hypothesis" was new and I did not know much about it. I asked her why she wanted to know.

She said: "I went to see Jody, (her internist) last week and he told me my cholesterol was too high and I needed to change my diet."

We talked a bit longer and I asked her what she was going to do. She indicated she was going to give it a try.

I happened to talk to her about three months later, and asked her how the diet was going.

She said: "I'm going to see Jody next week and tell him I'm not going to do this diet anymore. You know, I'm a widow lady now, and eating is the last pleasure I have in life."

Jody died of his heart attack a few years later. Grandmother died 25 years later at age 96.

———o———

Families get involved in the doctor's practice, and not just because the doctor is grumpy and irritable. I usually had my children answer the phone to run interference for me. Millie was a young girl who developed kidney failure, and took to calling the house practically every morning about 7AM. The kids got so good at it they could answer the phone, hear her ask for me and say: "Dad, its Millie."

Then one day the phone rang at 7 AM and it was not Millie, but her brother, who said: "Millie is lying on the floor and I can't get her to wake up."

I got on the phone and told him to hang up and call 911. Unfortunately, Millie was already dead. My children learned early on what the practice of medicine involved.

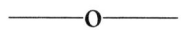

———o———

In those days we only had a beeper, so the answering service operator would sometimes try my home phone number first to save time. One Saturday afternoon, I was out in the garden using a tiller when my son came to the back door and gave me the universal hand signal that I had a call.

When I got to the phone, the operator was laughing. I asked what was so funny and she said: "I just have to know what you were doing. Your daughter told me you were out mowing the dirt."

———o———

We were eating lunch in the mess hall at the table where the doctors usually sat. The psychiatrist joined us and said, "I saw a really interesting patient today. She has this strange ritual where after supper she goes out into her back yard, goes to one particular area, and gets several spoons full of dirt, and eats it. She has been doing this for 30 years, but she does not appear to have any psychiatric problems I can find."

The diagnosticians at the table all said: "She has iron deficiency anemia." Known as pica, this is one of those strange medical phenomena. The most common form of pica occurs in pregnant women, usually those who are poorer and lacking social support, who become iron deficient and who eat large quantities of Argo® starch as a result. I do not know why it was always that particular brand—perhaps it was the cheapest or the most readily available at the grocery store. With better outreach on the part of public health departments, who routinely provide vitamin and iron supplements, this is not so common anymore.

I also saw one variation on this presented at Grand Rounds when I was in Birmingham. The patient presented with the clinical picture of massive iron overload. After considerable effort the people taking care of her were able to diagnose pica, except she had been eating the dirt in the Birmingham area, which is loaded with relatively insoluble, and therefore biologically useless, iron. After all, Birmingham became a steel center because iron and coal were both readily available.

———o———

The new resident was explaining to the old surgeon the new operation for peptic ulcers called "highly selective vagotomy." The surgeon expressed interest, but said: "I think I will stick with the operation I know. He proceeded to do a truncal vagotomy, (severing the nerve to the stomach), removed the lower half of the stomach known as the antrum, and started to work on freeing up the duodenum, the first part of the small intestine, with the intention of sewing it to the end of the stomach.

I was not really all that interested in the operation, but it seemed to be going slowly. Suddenly I became aware of tension in the room and that everything had stopped. Neither the resident nor I said anything. I could see there was a problem, but had no idea what it was or what to do.

Fortunately, the circulating nurse was an old pro—she looked into the wound and asked "Would you like me to call Dr. Buck?" The surgeon said he would.

Dr. Buck came into the room looked into the wound and asked what the problem was.

The surgeon explained: "I've already resected the antrum with the intention of doing a Billroth I anastamosis, but I could not free up the duodenum because of the scar tissue."

Dr. Buck said: "Why don't you just put a Foley in the duodenum and do a Billroth II?" (Sew the stomach to a portion of the small bowel downstream from the duodenum.) The surgeon said okay, and the operation went on to a successful conclusion.

I learned that once committed, you could not afford to lose your nerve, since stopping in the middle of the case was not an option. The trick is to balance the risks and benefits of a proposed course of action before you start. Once started you have to make the best of the situation as it develops.

———o———

I had occasion to recall this incident while I was deployed for three months to the Sinai peninsula as part of a peace-keeping mission. My group was charged with providing medical support to a battalion of U. S. paratroopers, who considered themselves particularly tough warriors. Their mission, though, consisted of being deployed in 8-10 man groups for 10 days at a time in strategic locations to watch and report any unusual activity. Needless to say, this duty involved long stretches of sheer boredom combined with primitive living conditions. The one hot meal daily was the high point. After 10 days they then rotated back to the base camp, where they had few duties, but a lot recreational opportunities as well as access to beer.

I was summoned to our facility, which consisted of a single room with five cots, two of which were occupied, to see the third young soldier. He had been brought in after suffering a head laceration from hitting a door during an episode of binge drinking following one of those 10 days stretches on a mountain top. He was agitated, and had his platoon sergeant and one of his buddies, both of whom were sober, hanging onto him and trying to keep him on the stretcher when I got there.

He kept saying: "My daddy's gonna whip my ass." This despite the fact that his platoon sergeant, and eventually his lieutenant, were all there, while Dad was back in the States.

I calmed the young man down, told him I needed to suture his laceration closed to stop the bleeding, and I needed him to hold still. He said he would, but as soon as I started, he started bucking again. This happened two more times, and I finally warned him: "If you don't hold still, I am going to have to give you something to put you down."

He didn't, I did, and finished sewing him up. His platoon leader asked me if I was going to bring charges against him for his behavior, since I was an officer, and the soldier had not done as he was told. I assured him I was a doctor first, and the course of action was up to him.

Dr. Lucius F. Wright

As I closed, one of the young paratroopers who had been "hospitalized" to get over his GI symptoms looked at me in a somewhat wide-eyed fashion and asked "Is it like this all the time?"

Clearly this was just like on television from his perspective. From mine, it was a welcome break from the monotony of doing nothing for days on end.

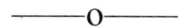

———o———

The paratrooper had fallen and landed on his thumb, breaking one of the bones. Even though I was board certified in nephrology, not orthopedics, I was the only doctor for 250 miles. Fortunately I had a text book of orthopedics and a cast technician, so I went about stabilizing the fracture and casting it while looking over my shoulder at the book.

About a week later, the soldiers were playing volleyball when one of them landed crookedly and sustained a compound fracture, meaning the bone was sticking out through the skin, of both bones in his lower leg. Clearly, this was an injury that required surgery, so we arranged for an ambulance to drive him to the Israeli hospital in Eilat. As they were loading the man into the vehicle, I saw the cast tech and told her: "Grab the trooper with the thumb and take him, too."

When the ambulance crew and tech got back later that evening I asked her what had happened to "the guy with the thumb."

She replied: "He told me to tell my orthopedist to increase the angle of distraction the next time." "I told him we didn't have an orthopedist, only a nephrologist and a family practitioner." He looked at me, laughed, and said: "Your Army is as crazy and mixed up as mine."

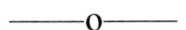

———o———

The tornado had touched down in Jackson, and I had responded by going to the Emergency Room. One of the nurse managers and I set up an ad hoc treatment area where those with less severe injuries could be sent and tended to, freeing up space in the Emergency Room.

He was a boy about eight years old who appeared to have been traumatized, but not injured, so he was sent to our area. Upon examination, though, it seemed to me that he probably had a ruptured spleen, so I ordered confirmatory X-rays. With the diagnosis established, I sent him back around to the ER for the surgeon to examine and prepare for surgery.

When things slowed down, I went back around to the ER to follow up on the boy. There was a large crowd of people in the room with him, including several nurses and therapists, who were trying to get the boy to tell them his name, so they could try to get consent for the surgery. The boy was awake, but saying nothing.

I decided to see what I could do, so I went up to the bedside and told him my name, again, and asked if he was hurting.

He shook his head, "No."

I then said: "What's your name? You look like a Bobby to me."

He said: "Its Jimmy."

I said: "Okay, Jimmy. Can you tell me your last name, too?

Before he could answer, several of the women around the bed started talking to him simultaneously, trying to get him to answer the question.

Finally, the surgeon said: "He was doing fine before you barged in. Why don't you all just hush and let him finish?"

I asked the question again and he told me. One of the people in the room recognized the name—his mother and sister had been dead on arrival.

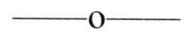

———o———

This is not the only instance where nurses failed to recognize that I might be able to talk to children. We had a meeting at Hilton Head attended by the management team of the dialysis unit. I took the crew out to dinner, along with their families. After dinner, one of the nurse managers sent her three year old daughter down to my end of the table to thank me for the dinner.

She was not shy, but it was noisy and I had some difficulty hearing her. I asked her if she wanted to sit in my lap and talk to me. She readily agreed, thanked me again for dinner, and then proceeded to tell me that her grandfather had "a wig." I made a production out of laughing at her story, then told her that I could see her mother was getting anxious about our conversation, and she should probably go back to her end of the table. She hopped down and did so.

I found out later that the members of the team who were sitting at the adjoining table were all amazed that I would pick a child up, put her in my lap and talk to her like I did. It took one of the old hands to point out this was not so mysterious, since I had plenty of practice talking to my four children.

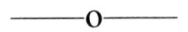

———o———

Some experts estimate half of what physicians do on any given day is of no "value." The problem, of course, is that we do not know which half is which.

Dr. Lucius F. Wright

My grandfather was a physician with expertise in the treatment of tuberculosis. He served as an Army physician from 1917 to 1945 and spent three tours at the Army's "TB" hospital in Denver. I had the privilege of doing residency training there 30 years later.

By the time I arrived, antibiotics effective in treating TB had been developed, deployed and the disease was considered curable. In my grandfather's time, a variety of treatments were used. For instance, the disease had a predilection to appear in the upper part of the lung, so surgeons would remove it. The germ thrived with high oxygen concentrations, so surgeons would collapse a disease lung, lowering the oxygen. There was even a time when ping-pong balls were placed into the cavity between the lung and the chest wall. None of these measures reliably cured the patient, yet some survived. In fact, I saw some of these patients.

At first I was shocked by the problems they were dealing with as a direct result of the efforts of the doctors of my grandfather's era. Then I came to realize that they were the survivors—did the treatment help? They were doing the best they could with the information available. We will likely always need more information. With this in mind consider these following stories, each an instance of a therapeutic misadventure.

———o———

Many commentators are decrying the death of the family doctor, the one you saw for everything. In my experience, that nostalgia is misplaced, as illustrated by a number of stories.

The patient was seen in the Emergency Department complaining of weakness. A workup showed that he had very low red blood cell counts, white blood cell counts, and platelet counts, but nothing to suggest leukemia. His working diagnosis was aplastic anemia, a commonly fatal illness. As part of my evaluation, I asked him about his medications, and he said his family doctor, Dr. Welby, had been giving him a shot for his arthritis.

Gold injections had been introduced as an experimental therapy for rheumatoid arthritis and its toxicity was not well understood, so I suspected this was the drug in question. To be sure, though, I called Dr. Welby the next morning, identified myself as the intern on his patient's case, and asked him if he remembered or could consult his records and tell me what injection he had been giving.

He was affable, paused while he looked it up, and said: "I've been giving him 1 cc of Anectine ® IM every month."

Since I was not familiar with the drug, I asked him to spell it, thanked him and told him I would make sure he got a copy of our findings when the patient went home. It turns out I did know the drug, but by its other name, succinylcholine. This drug was then, and still is used in the operating room to create muscle paralysis! Good old Doc Welby had heard it was a muscle relaxant and thought it would be a good treatment for his patient's pain, not realizing he might accidentally end of all of his pain, as most small offices were not equipped to provide life support if he stopped breathing.

The Michael Jackson incident is really not new, just better publicized. Doctors will often use drugs for purposes other than that for which they are intended, not fully recognizing the risks involved.

———o———

He was the first transplant patient I saw after moving to Jackson. He had come to the Clinic with his wife, who had a doctor's appointment. While sitting there, he noticed my name on a sign board. As he told me: "I thought, I haven't seen a nephrologist about my kidney transplant in years, so maybe I had better do that."

He then told me his family doctor had recently told him he had "pre-leukemia" and thought he was going to die from it soon. I asked him what had led to this and he said his "counts" were low. I did a complete blood count and sure enough, he was severely anemic and had a markedly suppressed white blood cell count. I asked him how long this had been going on and he said about three months. Further questioning disclosed that he had developed classic gout about 3 months previously and had started a new medication for this—allopurinol. This was a classic instance of a drug interaction causing an accidental overdose.

I explained to him that allopurinol blocks the metabolism of azathioprine, one of his main anti-rejection medications, resulting in an accidental overdose. I had him stop both drugs for ten days, and then had him restart the azathioprine in a lower dose and stop the allopurinol. This worked, and all of the abnormalities went away.

I followed him for another 25 years before he died of heart disease.

———o———

She had poorly controlled diabetes and developed kidney failure and near blindness as a result. Fortunately, her daughter donated a kidney to her. In those days the only medications available to prevent rejection of the transplant were azathioprine, an anti-cancer drug, and prednisone, which commonly causes people's blood sugar to go up.

She came in to see me for a regularly schedule visit. She told me she had been to see the new young family doctor who had just opened his practice in her little town. He saw her and decided the solution to the problem of controlling her diabetes was to stop the prednisone, which she had done less than a week ago. He failed to recognize that one drug alone was not likely to prevent rejection. Fortunately, we restarted the prednisone and she did not have problems with transplant rejection.

———o———

Today's medical care is more fragmented than ever, and I know patients miss some of the personal touch. But sometimes the personal touch can still work, even though in different ways than times past.

She had been a patient for several years, but finally got a transplant and moved to Texas. One afternoon I got a phone call from a transplant surgeon in Dallas. He said she was there, had rejected her kidney, and was now uremic. He had recommended starting her back on dialysis right away, but she wanted to put it off and come back to West Tennessee. She was sitting in the office with him, and he asked me if I would talk to her.

She was upset, partly because the rejection had occurred when she ran out of money and quit taking her medications. She wanted to come home, but was afraid I would not take her back.

I assured her I would reserve a spot for her, but she needed to let the surgeon take care of her. I pointed out that if she got sick on the bus ride back home, she would end up God knows where, and next time she might not get lucky enough to find a doctor who was comfortable calling from the big city medical center to some unknown place in the country for the "LMD" to talk to her.

———o———

I was attracted to internal medicine because of its "puzzle-solving" aspects, and have a fondness for the patient with the rare diagnosis. Truth be to tell, making the diagnosis is not usually a case of special brilliance on my part, but of simply paying attention. I want to end by giving a couple of good examples.

The cardiologist called me and asked me to see a patient he had admitted with an unusual form of heart failure, known as "high-output" cardiac failure. This is different from the usual forms in that the heart is pumping out plenty of blood, often too much, yet the patient is getting congested and filling up with fluid. There is a relatively short differential for this problem, and he had not been able to diagnose it.

I could not either. The patient's condition deteriorated fairly rapidly to the point where about midnight, I got a call that he was in trouble and I needed to dialyze him to remove some of the extra fluid.

I had him brought to dialysis and, as we started getting him ready for the treatment, his wife arrived. I talked to her, told her what we were doing, and mentioned we had not been able to figure out what was causing his problem in the first place.

She said: "Well this all started when he went to see old Dr. T, who gave him some drops for his cough and congestion."

Fortunately, I realized she had told me something important. I asked her if the drops were called "SSKI" and she said it was.

SSKI stands for soluble solution of potassium iodide, which was an old-time remedy that I have never had occasion to prescribe. Iodine is used in the body by the thyroid gland, and "thyroid storm" can be caused by administration of iodine—one of those rare medical conditions named for old professors, Jod & Basedow.

Thyroid storm is a recognized cause of high-output failure. Although the levels of his thyroid hormone had returned to normal by the time we measured them, treating him as thyroid storm "cured" his condition.

This story is proof of the old adage: "If you wait long enough and listen closely enough, the patient will tell you what is wrong with them."

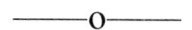

———o———

She was an elderly white woman brought to the Emergency Room by her husband one Sunday afternoon, who was convinced that she was "slipping away." She did appear somnolent and non-communicative, but there was nothing in her history or physical examination to explain the symptoms. She was taking very little in the way of medication.

Lacking a diagnosis, I cast a wide net by ordering laboratory tests, hoping for a clue. The pathology resident called me back about an hour later reporting her serum sodium concentration and serum chloride concentration were virtually identical. (Normally the chloride is about 40 units lower.) Since the lab results were biologically impossible, I asked him what might be interfering with the lab analysis. He thought about it a minute and said: "The test will pick up any halogen. Could it be bromine?"

AH HA! This was a clue. I went back and talked to her husband, and asked her if she was taking anything over the counter. After a moment, he said: "Yes, she has an old bottle of Miles Nervine® that she has been using."

This was an old formulation of bromide, which had long been used as a sedative. It was pitched as a mail order product beginning in 1935, and had actually been off the market for several years prior to this patient's appearance. She had been saving it up, because it worked so well. Another example of an "old bromide."

———o———

Dr. Lucius F. Wright

I hope the stories I have shared have been more than bromides—I hope they have encouraged you to think about your values and what you want to tell your doctors so he/she can do a better job helping you along the way.

Stories of Life

About the Author

Lucius F. Wright, M. D., received his B. A. from Vanderbilt University in 1970 and his M. D. from the University of Alabama School of Medicine in January 1974. He is board certified in internal medicine and the subspecialty of nephrology. He served in the U. S. Army Medical Corps from 1975 to 1983. Since 1983 he has practiced medicine with The Jackson Clinic Professional Association in Jackson, Tennessee. He has served that organization as Chairman of the Board of Directors, Medical Director, and currently as Chair for Quality Improvement. He received the Founder's Award from The Jackson Clinic in 2006, an honor established to recognized the high standards of clinical excellence and progressive medical practice established by the founders of the Clinic in 1950. He wrote or co-wrote both editions of *The History of the Jackson Clinic (1992 and 2000.)*

He has served as medical director for Dialysis Clinic, Incorporated, a non-profit organization providing dialysis

Stories of Life

services to patients in 27 states. He has served that organization in many roles, and has spoken often on the essential elements of leadership to achieve clinical excellence. In that role he has authored two editions of the company's *Medical Director's Handbook*.

He has served in numerous leadership positions at Jackson-Madison County General Hospital, including chairman of the Department of Medicine for three years, and as Chief of Staff from 2010-2012.

He has served on the Tennessee Renal Disease Advisory Committee for more than 20 years, and as chairman since 2010. He is a Fellow of the American College of Physicians, and a member of the American Society of Nephrology and the Renal Physicians Association, in addition to the local and state medical societies. He has been a representative on numerous statewide and national committees.

He is the author of a technical monograph, *Maintenance Hemodialysis*, two editions of the nephrology chapter in *Rakel's Textbook of Family Practice*, and 22 scientific papers involving both laboratory and clinical investigations.

He and his wife, Cynthia, live in Jackson, Tennessee, and have four adult children and four grandchildren. When not busy with medical activities, he is active in his church choir, is a founding member of The Jackson Choral Society, and pursues gardening.

Main Street Publishing, Inc.

206 E. Main Street, Suite 207
P.O. Box 696
Jackson, TN 38301

Toll Free #: 866-457-7379
or
Local #: 731-427-7379

Visit us on the web:
www.mainstreetpublishing.com
www.mspbooks.com

E-Mail: editor@mainstreetpublishing.com